W9-CFV-270

How to Deal with

AUTISM

Kids' Health™

Lynette Robbins

PowerKiDS press™

New York

For Danielle

Published in 2010 by The Rosen Publishing Group, Inc.
29 East 21st Street, New York, NY 10010

First Edition

Editor: Joanne Randolph
Book Design: Kate Laczynski
Photo Researcher: Jessica Gerweck

Photo Credits: Cover, p. 1 Titus Lacoste/Getty Images; p. 4 Sean Justice/Getty Images; p. 6 Shutterstock.com; p. 8 Toby Maudsley/Getty Images; p. 10 © Tom Stewart/Corbis; p. 12 © www.istockphoto.com/Yenwen Lu; p. 14 Bambu Productions/Getty Images; p. 16 © www.istockphoto.com/Monika Adamczyk; p. 18 Victoria Yee/Getty Images; p. 20 Ariel Skelley/Getty Images.

Library of Congress Cataloging-in-Publication Data

Robbins, Lynette.
    How to deal with autism / Lynette Robbins. — 1st ed.
        p. cm. — (Kids' health)
    Includes index.
    ISBN 978-1-4042-8142-4 (lib. bdg.) — ISBN 978-1-4358-3421-7 (pbk.) — ISBN 978-1-4358-3422-4 (6-pack)
    1. Autism in children—Juvenile literature. I. Title.
    RC553.A88R627 2010
    618.92′85882—dc22
                                        2009007862

Manufactured in the United States of America

CONTENTS

4

A Boy with Autism

Alex was a fussy baby. He cried a lot and did not like to be picked up or cuddled. Alex did not start talking until he was nearly two years old. By three, Alex was still using only one or two words at a time. Other children his age were speaking in sentences. He did not want to play with other children or even look at other people. He would also flap his hands when he got upset or excited. Alex spent a lot of time by himself.

Alex has autism. People who have autism are born with it. You cannot catch autism from someone else. There is no cure for autism, but there are ways to treat it.

New places or things can be too much for children with autism to handle. These children will often cry or scream when they feel this way.

What Is Autism?

Autism is a **disorder** of the brain. People with autism have trouble making sense of the world around them. It is hard for them to **interact** with other people. They have trouble understanding other people and what those people are feeling. It is also hard for people with autism to put their own thoughts and feelings into words.

People with autism may also be extra **sensitive** to their surroundings. Sounds may seem louder to them. Smells may seem stronger. Lights might seem brighter. A person with autism may not like being touched by other people. She may get very upset if there is too much happening around her.

People with autism may like to spend time alone rather than with other people. It is hard for them to understand others and connect with them.

7

Signs of Autism

Children with autism do not generally like to play with other children. They may not pay attention to the people around them. Children with autism often like to do one thing over and over. They may move a body part, such as their hands, all the time. They may repeat certain words. They may always play with the same toy or want the same lunch every day. They may not like it when they are forced to make a change.

Children with autism may seem to get upset for no reason. Loud noises or being touched can upset some people with autism. When children with autism get upset, they may throw **temper tantrums**. Some autistic children try to hurt themselves or others. It can be very hard to calm them down.

At first, other students thought Benny was strange because he often sat against the wall and rocked. Now they know that Benny acts that way because he has autism.

9

Everybody's Different

Every person who has autism is different. No two autistic people will have exactly the same **symptoms**. Some people have **severe** autism. A person with severe autism may not speak. He may not be able to do everyday tasks, such as dressing himself or using the bathroom by himself. He may do odd or upsetting things, such as bang his head against the wall or chew on furniture.

Other people have less severe symptoms. They may be able to learn to do things to take care of themselves. They may learn to read and write. However, it can take a very long time for autistic children to learn new things.

Even something that seems as simple as learning to tie your shoes can be hard for someone with autism. Some people may never learn to do these things.

Asperger's Syndrome

Asperger's syndrome is a type of autism. People who have Asperger's have less severe symptoms than most autistic people. People with Asperger's do not have trouble using or understanding words. Unlike most autistic people, they may be interested in other people. However, people with Asperger's still tend to have poor **social skills**.

Alan has Asperger's. He is interested in trains. He spends all his time learning and thinking about trains. Like Alan, people with Asperger's tend to get very interested in one thing. People with Asperger's may also sound strange when they talk. They may not change the **expression** in their voice.

Casey has Asperger's syndrome. She became interested in the piano when was very young, and now she spends much of her time playing it.

What Causes Autism?

No one knows exactly why some people are autistic. Scientists do know that autism runs in families. Parents who have one autistic child are more likely to have another one than parents who do not. They also know that more boys seem to have autism than girls.

Many scientists think that autism is caused when something goes wrong during pregnancy. Some studies have shown that women who smoke or who are very **stressed** during pregnancy are more likely to have autistic babies. A pregnant woman who has eaten or been around harmful substances, such as **mercury** or lead, may also be more likely to have an autistic baby.

Nobody knows for sure what causes autism, but a healthy start is important for any pregnancy. This woman is talking to her doctor about ways to keep her baby healthy. **15**

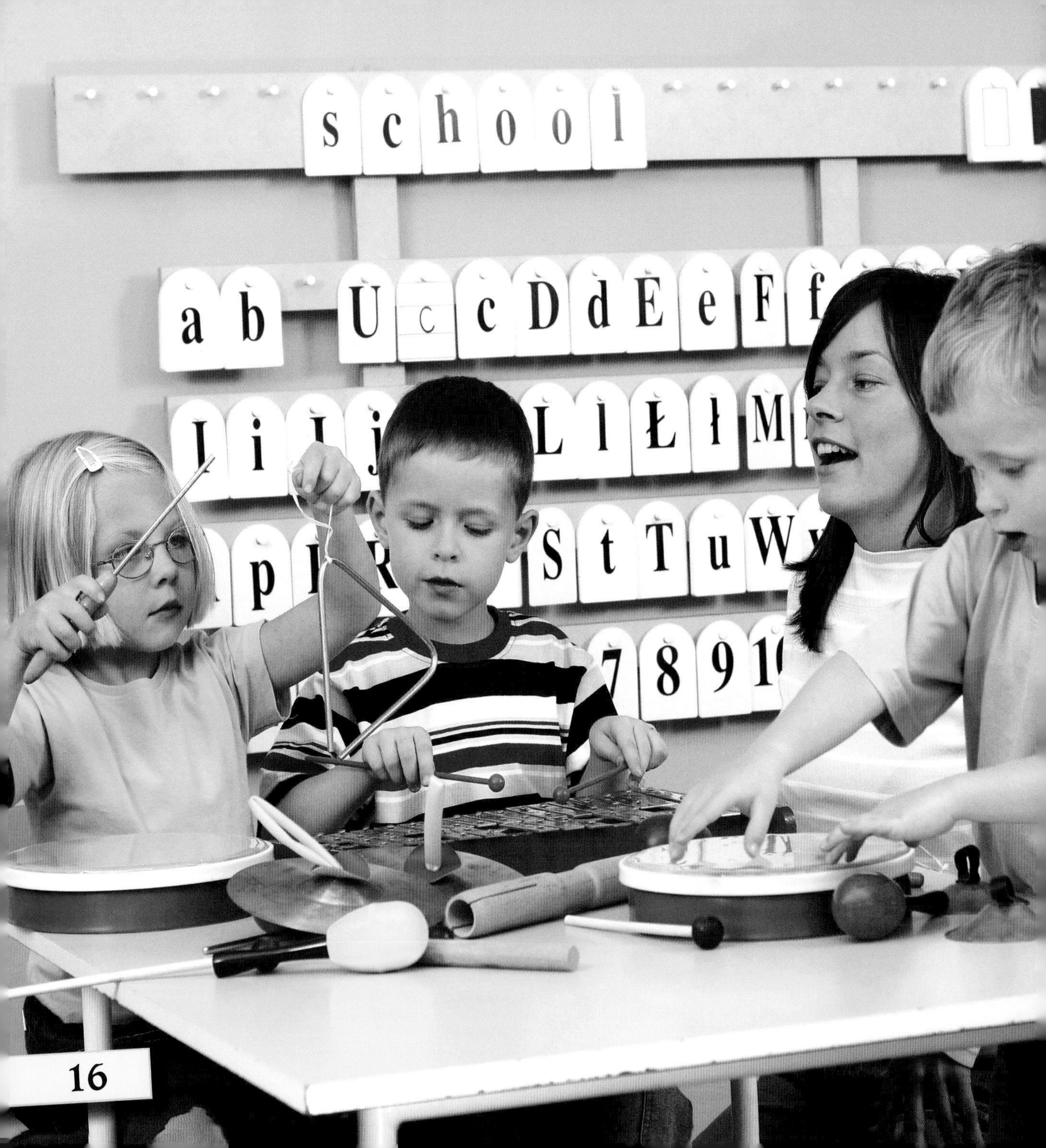
school

Treating Autism

Children with autism often behave in ways that other people find upsetting. These children cannot help it. One of the best ways to treat autism is to teach children how to get along with others and to care for themselves. It is best to start working with autistic children when they are very young. People who work with babies and young children with autism teach the children to look at them and to copy words and actions. This **therapy** must continue throughout their lives.

Some people think that changes in the kinds of food eaten and taking vitamins can help autistic children. There are also drugs that may help some symptoms.

Music therapy has been found to help many autistic children. Through music, these children are taught to use language better and change how they interact with others. **17**

Dealing with Autism

It can be very stressful to have a child with autism in the family. If the child has severe symptoms, he will need to be watched all the time. It may also be hard to take an autistic child to public places, such as parks or restaurants.

People with autism like **routine**. They like everything to be the same each day. People who take care of autistic children work hard to make sure that nothing upsets them. When something does upset an autistic child, it is important to calm him down quickly so that he will not hurt himself or the people and things around him.

Pet therapy has been shown to help people with autism. Therapy and service dogs, such as this one, are used to help autistic people build relationships and connect with people.

What if a Family Member Has Autism?

Katie's brother Eric has autism. Her parents spend all their time taking care of him. They are always tired. Katie helps take care of Eric, too. Katie feels sad because she does not get much attention from her parents. Katie loves her brother, but sometimes she wishes he did not have autism.

If you have a brother or sister with autism, you might feel sad like Katie. It is okay to feel sad sometimes. Autism has an effect on everyone in the family, not just the person with the disorder. It might help to talk to your parents about your feelings. Maybe they can find a way to spend some special time just with you.

Never be afraid to talk to your parents about how you are feeling. They may not realize you are feeling sad and left out if you do not tell them.

People who have autism need a great deal of attention. A person with severe autism will never be able to live on her own, even when she is grown up. She will always need someone to take care of her.

Many people with autism can grow up to take care of themselves. They can learn to talk with other people. They can learn to control themselves when something upsets them. It is best if they start to learn these things when they are very young. That is why families, teachers, doctors, and **therapists** are so important. Even though there is no cure for autism, people with this disorder can live happy, successful lives.

GLOSSARY

disorder (dis-OR-der) A sickness or medical condition.

expression (ik-SPREH-shun) A tone of voice that tells what someone is feeling.

interact (in-ter-AKT) To be around and talk with people.

mercury (MER-kyuh-ree) A poisonous, silver-colored element.

routine (roo-TEEN) When someone does something the same way over and over.

sensitive (SEN-sih-tiv) Can see or feel small differences.

severe (seh-VIR) Very bad.

social skills (SOH-shul SKILZ) Knowing how to get along well with others.

stressed (STREST) Worried or feeling bad because of a problem.

symptoms (SIMP-tumz) Signs that show someone is sick or has a disorder.

temper tantrums (TEM-per TAN-trumz) Fits in which a person becomes angry and loses control. The person may cry, kick, and scream.

therapists (THER-uh-pists) People who are trained to work with people to help them understand their feelings.

therapy (THER-uh-pee) The treatment of disorders or injuries.

INDEX

WEB SITES

Due to the changing nature of Internet links, PowerKids Press has developed an online list of Web sites related to the subject of this book. This site is updated regularly. Please use this link to access the list:
www.powerkidslinks.com/heal/autism/